perfect practice

How to zero in on your goals to see results faster

CHRISTIAN J. TRIOLA

An imprint of
Tenterhook Books, LLC
Akron, Ohio

Copyright © 2018, 2020 Christian J. Triola & Amy Joy Triola
All rights reserved.

Except as permitted under the U.S. Copyright Act of 1976, no part of this publication may be reproduced, distributed, or transmitted, in whole or in part, in any form or by any means, or stored in any form of retrieval system, without prior written consent of the author.

Cover Art and Book Design by Amy Joy, ©2018 Amy Joy

Library of Congress Control Number: 2020921871

ISBN-13: 978-1-953101-16-7

Contents

1. What is Practice?   1
2. Finding Time   5
3. Preparing to Practice   10
4. Setting Goals   16
5. Adding Variety   27
6. Adding Musicality   33
7. Don't Forget to Have Fun and Explore   39
8. The Value of Memorization   43
9. Creating your Personal Practice Plan   47
10. Ideas for Practice   54
11. Final Thoughts   59

What is Practice?

Since the late 90s, I've taught hundreds of guitar students, and most of them (including myself) have complained about the same problems:
1. I don't have **time** to practice
2. I don't know **what** to practice
3. I don't feel **inspired** to practice

These same three problems come up time and again, so chances are, at some point, you've caught yourself saying these same things.

On top of that, most students don't really understand what it means to practice. For many people, we think of practice as the repetition of the same sort of thing over and over again in an attempt to improve a skill. However, practice is much more complicated than that. Repetition can only get you so far. You have to be engaged with it. You have to have goals, a reason for practicing. Otherwise you end up just going through the motions, resulting in little to no measurable results. This will inevitably lead to frustration, boredom, and eventually a loss of interest in something that you once loved doing so much.

> **"Repetition can only get you so far. You have to have goals, a reason for practicing. Otherwise you end up just going through the motions, resulting in little to no measurable results."**

So how do we overcome this? Well, that's what this book is intended to help you do: to overcome the obstacles in your way of getting quality consistent practice.

THE FIRST STEP

The first step is to get a better understanding of what it means to practice. For a lot of people, they know they want to practice, in fact they may even pick up their guitar intending to practice, but then they just kind of review their favorite things, run out of ideas, set the guitar down and go do something else. They feel better, but they haven't really practiced. What

> **"Good practice should get you thinking about what it is you are doing."**

they've done is a simple review, which is a good thing to do as well, but it isn't practice.

Practice is more intentional than that. Practice has an end goal in mind. Good practice should get you thinking about what it is you are doing. When you practice well, you should be fully engaged with whatever it is you are trying to do. As such, practice is different from rehearsal. **Rehearsal** is preparation for a performance, which means you are applying what you learned in practice so that it is ready for others to finally hear it. Therefore, *practice* can be defined as time spent in order to improve, refine, or review specific skills you wish to develop.

So now that we have a clearer definition of what practice is, let's work on overcoming our first obstacle: finding the time.

CHAPTER 1 RECAP:
1. **Practice is not the same as rehearsal.** Practice is dedicated time spent to improve, refine,

and review specific skills.
2. **Set goals for your practice.** Goals lead to measurable results.

Finding Time

Over 25 years ago, when I was first learning guitar in my early teens, I would rush home from my Saturday morning guitar lessons eager to practice. I would be consumed for the next several hours working on whatever it was I had just learned. I remember one Saturday, after only my second or third lesson, playing through "Jingle Bells" ad nauseam. I could hear some improvements as I practiced, but I didn't quite have it yet. Somewhat frustrated by my lack of progress, I put the guitar down. The next day I tried again. I was happy to hear that it sounded better than it had the day before. Then as I continued practicing it throughout the week, there would be days where it sounded flawless to my ears, and days where I kept messing it up. However, by the next Saturday, I was ready. And it sounded good when I played it for my teacher. I realized quickly that you don't always see the results of your practice right away, so I devoted as much time as I could to practicing the guitar.

But then the holidays came, and my Saturday afternoon practice schedule fell apart. On top of that, homework was piling up as the year was coming to an end. I started watching my coveted practice time slip away. But once the holidays were over and things returned to normal, I was able to get back to it. But then later that school year, I got a job and soon my evenings and Saturdays were booked. My practice schedule was now reduced to a few minutes here and there.

But I still loved my guitar, and I resented anything that got in the way of me playing it. So eventually I did something that I'd find out later is what every music teacher suggests: practice at the same time every day. However, since my high school and work schedules took up so much time and were rarely consistent, I had to get a little creative. So instead, I made sure that I knew when I was going to practice each day. Often, I'd schedule twenty minutes before and after work. Other times, I'd schedule in a break from homework to be sure I had time for some kind of practice.

It worked. All I needed to do was it make it part of my daily routine. I figured that

"Ten to fifteen minutes of daily, focused practice can be more effective than hours of practice in a single day."

since I showered and ate every day, why not play guitar too? At the time, I wasn't practicing for as long as I would have liked, but I was still progressing, still getting better.

WORK PRACTICE INTO YOUR ROUTINE

That's the thing about practice: ten to fifteen minutes of daily, focused practice can be more effective than hours of practice in a single day.

So that's the first thing you'll need to do: work practice into your daily routine. Make it such a part of your life that skipping practice would feel the same as skipping a meal or a shower.

The second thing is to figure out how much time each practice session will be. It would be ideal to do at least one to two hours a day, but that's not always practical. Remember that even ten focused minutes can have outstanding benefits.

The third thing, which will be discussed in more detail later in the book, is to always know what you will be practicing the next day.

TIME TO GET CREATIVE

It may not be easy to find your practice time at first, and you may have to get creative. Consider this: I have a guitar student who works full time, has two young children, and a new house. So he takes a guitar with him to work every day. On his lunch break, he eats and then spends the rest of the time practicing. And he's been making fantastic progress quite quickly, despite the fact he rarely gets to practice at home!

CHAPTER 2 RECAP:

1. **Work practice into your daily routine.** Make it a habit like taking a shower or brushing your teeth.
2. **Set the amount of time you will practice each day.** Anywhere from 5 minutes to 5 hours, depending on the day and what is practical.
3. **Always know what you are going to practice.** Create a plan for your next practice session before ending your routine.

4. **Be consistent.** Daily, consistent practice is more beneficial than sporadic practice. Ten minutes every day is more beneficial than one day a week for several hours.

Preparing to Practice

Of course, grabbing your guitar, working on a few measures, a riff, or a song isn't quite enough either. You also have to approach your practice with the right frame of mind to get the most out of it.

To some degree, you do have control over this. However, fatigue, stress, and other outside factors can pollute your attempts to practice. When this happens, sometimes it's best to put the guitar down and take a break. Forcing yourself to practice when your mind or body needs rest can actually hurt your practice session.

On the other hand, don't use being a little tired as an excuse not to practice. Just know that there may be factors outside of your control that can limit how well your practice session can go.

SET UP YOUR PRACTICE SPACE

That said, there are factors you can control. First is how well you set up your practice space. A good practice space should have as few distractions as possible. It should be quiet and allow for the best possible means of concentration. You should have a music stand, pencil, metronome, tuner, and a comfortable chair, preferably without arms. Also around you should be a way of listening to music. I'd recommend a tablet or desktop computer. It's always a good idea to hear what it is you are working on whenever you can. Even if you don't read music and prefer to play by ear, having a music stand can be a valuable piece of equipment to have handy. You can keep lists of songs, ideas, and other aids to memory that can help you focus your practice time.

> *"A good practice space should have as few distractions as possible."*

FOCUS

The second factor you can control is your frame of

mind. Before practicing you'll want to ask yourself: "How will I improve today?" This simple question can help you to focus your practice almost instantly. There are millions of things you could practice, from whole songs, to scales, to techniques, so simply asking yourself how you want to improve in that practice session will help you figure out what to work on. But the trick is not to simply answer with the name of a song or a technique. You'll want to be much more specific than that.

> **There are millions of things you could practice. To see results, make your practice goals as specific as possible.**

For example, let's say your teacher assigned you to practice strumming the chords of a song you want to learn, but you've only just learned the chords. Instead of trying to learn the whole song by struggling through it, focus on only one new chord. Make it your goal for that day to be able to somewhat comfortably grab that new chord without hesitation. Make sure you know that chord by the time your practice time is up. If you have more time, you may try to include a second or third chord. But you don't have to try and learn them all in one day. Always break down what you want to learn and then learn it one item at a time. The longer you play, the more material you'll be able to fit into that one item, so instead of one chord, you may be able to memorize an entire chord progression. But again, that comes with time and knowing your fundamentals.

PRACTICE POSITIVE SELF-TALK

Additionally, besides asking yourself the focusing question, you will also want to remind yourself that this is something you can, in fact, do. Don't let negative self-talk get in the way of good practice. And don't let others discourage you. Most of the time, the people who hear you practicing don't realize that you are working to get better, not performing for their enjoyment. So don't let them grind you down or make you think you're not any good. Everyone who starts learning an instrument sounds bad at first. This is normal.

*"***S**ometimes you just have to say to yourself, 'I am good at this. I can figure this out.'"*

It takes a while to gain physical control over all the elements involved in playing the guitar. Sometimes you just have to say to yourself, "I am good at this. I can figure this out." It may sound strange to say that, but it works. It helps to motivate you as well as silence any naysayers.

Self-doubt is a big obstacle when it comes to playing any instrument (or writing a book, or creating a work of art, or anything that is subjected to subjective judgement). So you'll want to remember, practice is the time to make mistakes. It's the time to experiment. It's the time to figure it out. It's the time to get your fingers well-trained to obey your instant mental commands. And this takes time. Also, you'll have great practice sessions where your mind is clear, your heart is in it, and your fingers can do no wrong.

Bad practice days happen to everyone. They aren't a measure of talent or ability.

And then there are days where your head is foggy, you don't feel like you care, and your fingers have magically turned into dolphin fins and you can't seem to play anything right. When this happens, just remember: it happens to everyone. It is in no way a measure of talent or ability. It's just a bad day.

CHAPTER 3 RECAP:
To Prepare for Practicing:
1. **Set up your practice space**: music stand, chair

or stool, pencil, metronome, tuner, etc.
2. **Know what your goals are for that day.** Be specific!
3. **Do whatever you need to get into the right frame of mind.** Put away all distractions for your allotted practice time.
4. **Quiet the negative self-talk.** It'll only work against you.
5. **Ask yourself: "How am I going to improve today?"** Using this focusing question will help you narrow your goal to something tangible.

Tip:
Don't keep your guitar in its case when at home. Instead, get an instrument stand or wall hanger and keep your guitar stored there. That way it's always visible and easily accessible. Often times, for guitar players, a guitar shut away in a case keeps them from seeing it, and therefore, it keeps it out of their hands. If you see it, you'll play it.

Setting Goals

It may sound strange, but I've had a lot of students who aren't really sure why they want to learn guitar, they just do. They like the look of it, or the sound, but they can't say for sure why they were attracted to the guitar and not the drums, piano, or some other instrument. And as such, many new players aren't sure what they want to be able to do with the instrument. Though it can be fun to just try it out for a while and see where it goes, once you've decided to do this for the long term, you'll need to set some goals to keep yourself both motivated and progressing.

Of course, not everyone comes to the guitar like

this. Some do have some kind of goal in mind. Some just want to strum along to their favorite songs. Some want to be in a band. Some are just hoping that it may impress a member of the opposite sex. And some decide that music is the life for them and that guitar is the instrument they simply can't resist. Whatever your reason was when you first began, you wanted to achieve your goal. Understanding what your long-term goals are can help you figure out what steps you can take today to get there.

THE FUNDAMENTALS

That said, there is one specific goal that all guitar players should strive for: to conquer the fundamentals, which include things like understanding notes, chords, scales, keys, technique, tone, and rhythm. These are the basic elements that will allow you to play a vast variety of music on the guitar, regardless of your approach to it. (Approach meaning whether you read music, learn by ear, by rote, or by TAB, or a combination of these.) Therefore, when you begin learning guitar, these are the elements that should

Every guitar player should seek to master the fundamentals.

fill up a majority of your practice time.

There are many places where you can find material in order to do this. There are countless books, videos, magazines, blogs, and apps. But where to begin? The fact of the matter is that they all have good information. Rarely have I come across instructional materials that didn't do what they promised. That said, much of this stuff can become confusing or overwhelming for beginners. So the best thing to do is keep looking until you find something that works for you.

> **When you begin learning guitar, the fundamentals should fill the majority of your practice time.**

For example, another one of my books, which is a favorite among my students, is **Guitar Chords Made Easy**. They love it because it takes them step-by-step through learning chords, and it was designed to make learning chords as easy as possible. It works because not only does it help them develop their fundamentals, but it also helps them achieve some of their goals!

This is the kind of thing you'll want to discover for yourself: what materials are going to make things clear and understandable while being fun and helping you master the fundamentals?

HOW TO CHOOSE YOUR DAILY GOAL

Choosing what to practice is vital in your development as a guitar player. By always knowing what it is you are going to try and improve on, you'll be able to notice progress more quickly. So before you sit down to practice, get in the habit of asking yourself the question mentioned in the last chapter: how am I going to improve today? The answer to that question will help you figure out what your main goal is going to be.

> "**B**y always knowing what it is you are going to try and improve on, you'll be able to notice progress more quickly."

For beginners, for example, your goal for one day might be to simply memorize where your fingers go for a new chord you are learning. For more advanced players, you might be trying to work out a new lick, and your goal for the day is to simply figure out the fingering for that lick and be able to play it at a slow tempo. The smaller your goal, the better. The more lofty your goal, the more time you'll need to accomplish it. So if you have the time, make your goals bigger, but always keep them manageable. If you don't, you'll quickly find yourself frustrated. If you find your goal is too big once you start it, stop and reassess. There is nothing wrong with scaling back your goal if needed.

Some might say, that sounds good, but taking things step-by-step like that is too slow. I want to get better faster. If you find yourself saying that, then you've discovered your goal. And the only way to get better faster is with more focused practice time.

Some days it may feel too taxing to force yourself into such focused concentration. On those days when you are tired or having trouble concentrating for whatever reason, instead of trying to improve, ask yourself this question instead: What would be the most satisfying thing to work on? In this case, your goal is to find something you enjoy doing but still needs some improvement, and spend your time on that. It doesn't matter if it's a few measures, a favorite song, or a simple scale, sometimes this type of practice can work to help you both enjoy what you are doing while helping to maintain your skills. This type of practice won't help you improve much, but it will allow you to keep your previously practiced skills up.

TAKE TIME TO REFLECT

One approach to setting your goals is to figure out what it is you want to internalize. The best way to do this is to make it a point to learn or memorize something new every practice session, even if that thing is just one single note.

Another part of your practice that you'll want to include is a moment or two for reflection. This is when you put the guitar down and ask yourself: what am I already good at? What do I need to work on? Are my hindrances physical, mental, or intellectual? By taking time to think about these things, you are essentially preparing for your next practice session. If time is limited in your next session, then make sure you focus right away on the things you need to work on. If you have more time, then perhaps you could start off with the thing you are good at to build confidence before going into the new material or review.

> "We are often so focused on improvement that we don't take the time to look at what we are doing well."

Now let's break down those questions. First,

what am I already good at? This is something most musicians, writers, artists, dancers, actors, etc., usually overlook. We are often so focused on improvement that we don't take the time to look at what we are doing well. By doing so, we become more aware of our areas of strength. This can help us in two ways: 1.) We will know with certainty how we might easily contribute to a band or group. If you know you're good with chords, for example, then it would be easier to play rhythm guitar in a band. 2.) It helps us understand our weaknesses better. You can't really know your weaknesses until you understand their opposite: your strengths. The better you understand one, the deeper understanding you start to get for the other.

> "**You can't really know your weaknesses until you understand their opposite: your strengths.**"

Second, are my hindrances physical, mental, or intellectual? Or in other words, what specifically is keeping me from accomplishing my goals?

For beginners, many times the problems are physical. They understand what they need to do, but their hands simply won't do them. This is overcome with time and focused practice. It takes a while for your hands to learn to quickly obey the new precise messages you are sending them. If you find that the physical act of playing to be a hindrance, then you'll want to focus on songs and exercises that will help you build finger strength and dexterity.

If your problem is mental, that means you are finding it difficult to concentrate for some reason. This usually happens when you are bored with whatever it is you're playing or trying to learn. When this happens, shift to something new, something you've never tried before. (Or in some cases, even try out a new instrument for a change of pace.) If you mostly play rock, try some jazz. If you mostly play country, try punk rock. Even if you don't necessarily listen to a lot of different music, give it a try. I know plenty of guitar players who don't really listen to metal, for example, but they love to play it. By exploring something brand new, you get yourself motivated and it helps you to better understand your instrument.

> **E**xploring something brand new can help get you motivated and help you better understand your instrument.

Now, if your problem is intellectual, that means for whatever reason, you just don't understand what you are doing, or in some cases why you are doing it. For example, if you usually learn songs from TABs, you may find learning to read notes a burden. However, there is much to be gained by doing so. So figure out why. Take the time to learn what you don't quite understand. And feel free to ask for help. There are plenty of music theory lovers out there who would be more than happy to help you.

Once you understand your hindrances, your strengths and weaknesses, you can then begin to work out a schedule for yourself that will help you to overcome your problems, harness your strengths, and develop your weaknesses so that they are no longer an issue.

> "Take the time to learn what you don't quite understand."

STAYING THE COURSE

After you get into the habit of establishing goals for yourself, the next thing you'll want to do is figure out how to maintain them and keep them consistent. It's fun to set goals. It makes you feel in-control, like you're getting somewhere. It's easy to start goals for similar reasons. However, it can be difficult to keep them going and see them through to completion. One reason for this is that we simply lose interest along the way—we still want the end result, but getting there isn't as exciting as we hoped it would be. So, how can you overcome this? By keeping everything you're doing as fresh as possible so that it feels new, even when it's day 458 and you've played the same scales for at least 450 of those days. To do this, keep your goals up to date, and keep them changing. Your brain will get bored with the same old stuff, so you have to keep things interesting for yourself. The changes don't have to be big either. For a scale you've played too many times, for example, see how fast you can play it, or play it in a different octave. Avoid getting into ruts. Each day ask yourself: how can I make tomorrow's practice both fun and even more productive than today?

CHAPTER 4 RECAP:
1. Set both long-term and short-term goals for yourself.
2. Keep your daily practice goals as specific as possible.

3. Make it a point to learn or memorize something new every day, even if it is just a single note.
4. Reflect on your practice session to help you discover your strengths, weaknesses, and anything that may be an obstacle to your goals.
5. Change, adapt, and revise your goals as often as you need to in order to keep it interesting so you can see them through to completion.

Adding Variety

The best way to get good at something is to do it every day. You see this clearly with infants. They are developing their motor skills to be able to do simple things like bring a spoon to their mouths without getting food all over their faces or bibs. They try it at each meal, and over time it becomes so second nature that they don't even think about it. Learning to play any instrument works the same way. The first step, besides understanding how the instrument produces sound, is to overcome your own physical limitations. And the best way to do that is through repetition.

However, this is where things get complicated.

The act of doing the same thing over and over again can both be positive and get you the results you're looking for, but it can also hinder your progress if you aren't mindful and precise in your practicing. In other words, just doing something over and over again won't make you a better player if you are practicing something incorrectly or start to zone out while doing it. So to avoid this, you need to add variety to your practice sessions.

CHANGE THINGS UP

Years ago, I learned how to tie together scales and arpeggios by practicing them using a modified version of the popular CAGED system. However, this version of the system was taught by jazz great Jimmy Bruno on a series of home videos I got from the library. I played these scale patterns with their accompanying arpeggios every time I practiced. It became my warm-up. At first they were revolutionary. I was understanding the fretboard better and my fingers were getting used to common patterns quickly. After a while, however, it became nothing more than a mindless exercise that had little benefit. Once I noticed this, I changed it to make sure that I did the exercises in a different key every day. That way, at the very least, I'd practice the same physical motions, but they'd be focused on a new set of notes every 12 days (one key per day). That simple change made it fresh, so I once again was focused and the practice was meaningful.

Of course, after a while, even having these exercises on a 12 day cycle grew stale, so I began skipping them entirely. But what I discovered is that I knew them very well. I'd internalized them. So my next step would be to find something new to use as a warm-up. And so I did. I started working on speed drills, then licks, then picking technique, then modes, different forms of minor, etc. And now when I practice, I have a variety of warm-ups to choose from.

> **Simple changes can make things fresh so your practice can once again become fresh and meaningful.**

AVOID PRACTICE BURNOUT

What I've learned is that each day you practice should be a little different from the last. You want repetition, but you don't want to wear out. Therefore, there are two things you can do for yourself that will help you prevent practice burn-out. First, just like weight lifters, give each practice day a focus.

For example, weight lifters have leg day or arm day or cardio day. Guitar players should have something similar, depending on your playing style or goals. For example: Monday—scale day, Tuesday—arpeggio day, Wednesday—lick day, Thursday—sweep picking day, Friday—fret hand technique day, etc. That way you don't overload yourself with one technique, but you do get a chance to work with each of them each week. And don't forget, once one of them gets old, find a way to change it up: try it in a new key, new octave, new speed, etc.

For example, when I was learning to play jazz, I played the most common jazz chord progression the ii-V-I in every key, every single day. Once it got old, I did the same progression, but with new voicings. Then I'd continue to change and mix up the voicings until I had a mastery over the chords. So now to warm up on chords, I'll find a jazz standard I know well and change the key and the voicings to challenge myself to discover something new while I warm up.

I find adding variety to your warm-up time is the best place in your practice session to start adding variety. There are countless ways to warm-up, so this part of your practice session should never get boring. The main purpose of the warm-up is to get your hands ready to take on any challenge you plan on presenting yourself that day, but it can also be used to learn something new at the same time. Some days your warm-up will be a minute or two, and other times it could last an hour or more, depending on your goals.

The second thing you'll want to do to avoid practice burn-out is to always seek out new things to play. If you hear something you like: try to learn it.

Tips:
1. Use technique exercises as a warm-up.
2. Apply the technique to a song or something you're learning.
3. Do them every day until you are no longer seeing the benefits.
4. Set an end date for the exercise so you don't just do it indefinitely. This will also give you a goal to accomplish.
5. Once you've mastered a technique, move on to something new.
6. Go back and review older technique exercises every now and again to make sure you can still do them.

Note: Variety doesn't end with warm-ups and technique exercises; it can also be applied to songs. Though repetition is key to learning a song, you'll want to focus on something new every day. That something new can be as small a few notes, or as long as a whole song.

CHAPTER 5 RECAP:

1. Balance repetition with variety.
2. Avoid repeating bad habits.
3. Each practice session should be a little different each day.
4. Use your warm-up time to work on techniques.

Adding Musicality

We play music to express ourselves. We want others to understand how we feel. But it's more than that. It's more than just feelings and emotions. Music can express states of mind, states of being, and its job is to make the listener feel that way too, or at least remind them of those feelings, thoughts, or states of being. But practice is often cold. There's a music-less click of the metronome, the concentration of getting the right notes at the right time, the desire to impress. However, none of that matters if you can't get your listener to feel something. And that's why you should always take time to add musicality to your practice, to make it come alive, to turn a mundane major scale into a thing that connects with a listener.

Your first step to understanding how to add this element to your practice is to ask yourself: why? Why did you choose to play this particular piece of music? The answers most people would give is: 1. I love the way it sounds, or 2. My teacher is making me play it, or 3. I need to learn it for a gig. If it is your choice to learn the song, there has to be a good reason for it. And once you know and understand your reason, that's when the music starts to happen. If you are being told to play it by a teacher or band member, then find something in it that you find worth sharing with others.

> **Music is expressive. Technical ability is meaningless without musicality.**

There are tricks and techniques that can be learned that help you to add expressiveness to your playing, but ultimately, listeners can tell when you are going through the motions. In fact, in many cases people enjoy listening to someone who is expressive, even if they aren't as technically sound, more so than a virtuoso whose playing is mechanical.

That said, there are many different approaches to adding musicality to your playing. The first way to do this is to get yourself in the right mindset before starting a piece of music. I've heard many players talk about what they think about before performing a piece of music. Many of them will have certain people they care about come to mind before they play to add an emotional dimension to their performance. Others will go deep and do their best to feel the way the song is supposed to feel. They may imagine a scene or place that allows them to connect to the music, making it more than just sound, but rather an expression of their ideas of what nuanced, emotional states sound like. And this is no easy task. It takes work. It takes dedication. It takes practice.

ADDING MUSICALITY TO YOUR PRACTICE

To add this element into your practice, first choose a song that you've played recently from beginning to end (or part of a song if you are still a beginner.) Second, hear the notes you are about to play in your mind. Know what you want it to sound like. Third, set your emotional dial. You don't want to think in terms of just happy or angry. There are many subtle levels of emotional states that have no names. Know how those states feel. Think of someone or something to help you understand this abstract feeling. Then begin. Fourth, once you've finished playing, reflect. Did it feel right? Did the song sound the way you feel it should? If you had an audience, do you think they would connect to it?

If you aren't sure how to make this happen, don't worry. It comes with time and a certain degree of mastery over your instrument. However, there are things you can do to help you achieve this kind of control over your playing. When you practice scales, for example, think of your instrument as a human voice. When notes get higher, the voice needs more breath and therefore gets louder. Do the same with the guitar. As your notes get higher, get louder. As you go lower, get softer. If you play with sharp, quick notes that don't last long, listen to how that affects you. How can you use that sound to evoke emotion? Then do the opposite. What do long, drawn out notes sound like to you? For me they sound like longing or wailing, but that's me. What do you make of it? How can you use them to create atmosphere or emotion?

Guitar players, of course, have a wide range of expressive tools at their disposal. Not only can you control how a note or chord is played, but you can also control the tone. For electric players, you can buy countless effect pedals, each one offering some new tone to explore and exploit. These are like adding colors to your palate. Learn how others utilize these pedals. Copy some of your favorites, but then discover your own tones. For acoustic players, strum the strings at different parts of the neck, add percussive hits, try different strings, different picks, whatever you can think of that will change the sound to what you want it to sound like. Doing so will help you connect more deeply and personally with your instrument, and result in a stronger performance. Use your practice time to discover what you sound like.

Tip:

Before reviewing a song you know well, ask yourself these types of questions: why are you playing this song or piece of music? Is it just for the sake of personal improvement or do you connect with it in some way? How can you add personal expression into your music? What techniques do you already know that can help you achieve this?

CHAPTER 6 RECAP:

1. Make it a point to add an element of musicality to your practice sessions.
2. Ask yourself: what is the core emotion I'm hoping to evoke with this song (or partial song)?
3. How can I add nuanced abstract states of being to my playing?
4. Include techniques in your practicing that helps you to add expressiveness to your playing.

Don't Forget to Have Fun and Explore

In the midst of trying to remember everything, one thing we often forget in our practice is to have fun and simply explore. This is your time to play with your instrument. Feel free to mess up as much as you'd like. Give yourself permission to get things wrong. Go ahead and break the rules. See what works and what doesn't.

Even though your main goal for any practice session should be improvement, you need to include play-time. During this part of your practice session, usually after you've worked hard to develop your skills, you need to relax and enjoy. You can play songs you like; you can write a new song, lick, riff, or chord progression. Or you can spend time figuring out what all those knobs do on your amp. This is the stage where you get to experiment. By doing so, you can discover a lot about your playing. What comes naturally? What sounds do you enjoy? Do you do too much of the same things? How can you do things differently this time? How can you get new sounds from your effect pedals? What happens when you pick with a quarter instead of a plastic pick? Find out. You may love it. You may hate it. Either way, you're discovering something new.

Music is bound by sets of agreed upon rules, but sometimes when those rules are broken, it becomes part of the ever-widening set of rules. For example, hundreds of years ago the sound created when you play a C followed by an F# was thought of as out of tune. In fact, it sounded so bad to them that they called it "the devil in music." However, as time went on composers started utilizing that sound and now it's so common, you wouldn't think it sounds out of tune at all. Musicians like Duke Ellington,

Broken rules today can become the new standard tomorrow. Experiment and see what you get.

Claude Debussy, Charlie Parker, Jimi Hendrix, and John Lennon all broke the rules. They all went with what they felt sounded good; sometimes it worked beautifully, but not always. They found dud sounds as well as plenty of innovations. But their approach wasn't random. It was intentional. It was based on what they heard in their heads. They were all trying to take what was inside them and let it out, and in doing so they discovered sounds and ideas that are used commonly today.

When I was in high school, I thought I'd discovered backward recording and circular picking. Turns out others had been doing both long before I was born. But for a moment, I felt like a genius. But I would have never discovered such things had I not taken the time to experiment.

CHAPTER 7 RECAP:

1. In each practice, don't forget to include time to experiment, explore, and have fun.
2. Through exploring you will not only get to know your instrument better, but you might just discover something new and spectacular.

Tip:

Take what you know and turn it upside down. Try to play a song backwards, for example. Add notes to a scale. Take notes out of a scale. Add and subtract notes from chords and see what happens. Take an open chord and move it up the neck. Take a jazz tune and turn it into a rock song. Take a rock song and make it reggae. If you don't know how to just yet, don't worry about it. Just take what you do know and play with it, experiment and see what you get.

The Value of Memorization

When I first learned how to play, I was taught by a guy who was classically trained, and as such, I was taught to read music. I didn't know that there were other ways of learning the guitar, so I did what I was told. I enjoyed reading the music, but the downside of it was that I never bothered to memorize anything other than what the notes looked like when I saw them on paper. As a result, by the time I joined my first band, I practiced and performed with a music stand with sheet music on it! Everyone else was playing without it. I felt a bit out of place. We were playing 90s alternative rock and there I was with Nirvana, Pearl Jam, and Green Day books sitting on the stand. If the book closed on me, I was done.

I'm not saying that learning to read music is a bad thing by any means. In fact, there is plenty of value in developing that skill, and I encourage everyone who learns guitar to learn to read music at some point. What I was missing, however, was a simple step that could have helped me tremendously. All I needed to do was **memorize** the songs.

INTERNALIZE THE MUSIC

Since that time, and as a result of my former dependence on sheet music, I encourage everyone who plays to internalize the music. Be able to play without anything in front of you. If you can, memorize everything you play: your warm-ups, your scales, modes, songs, licks, chord progressions. In fact, the act of practicing should partially be the act of memorization.

> "**The act of practicing should partially be the act of memorization.**"

If someone tells you to play a 12-bar blues in C (relative to your experience level) you should be able to do it from memory without having to sit and write it out.

I currently have a bass student who plays great. After years of playing electric bass, he bought an upright bass, which he figured out himself. I was impressed with what he was able to do on his own. He reads bass clef really well, but you take away that sheet music and he has no idea what to do with himself. I've been working with him to help him learn how to memorize, and so far so good, but it's a real problem for him at this point, something that might have been avoided had he begun practicing memorization sooner.

Another former guitar student now plays out regularly with a band. He's their singer and rhythm player. But he has a music stand with a tablet on it. As he plays the songs, he has the music going by on an app. Now there is nothing wrong with that if you need to do so. But the music he has memorized simply sounds better. He's more in control of it, and it shows.

CHAPTER 8 RECAP:
1. Memorization frees you from sheet music and puts you more in control of the music.
2. Incorporate memorization into your practice.

> **Tip:**
>
> Memorize everything. Learn tunes, licks, progressions. Be able to pick up your instrument and play a dozen or so songs simply from memory. Use the sheet music and tab to learn the songs and then put them away. Internalize the music.

Creating your Personal Practice Plan

Perfect practice means practicing with intent, having goals, and working toward them. It also means doing the best you can to play as consistently as possible. Make every note count. Make every moment count. Stay focused. And get ready to see results.

In order to do this, you'll want to put a practice plan in place. I recommend writing it out and keeping it on a music stand or with your guitar. Be sure to read it before every practice and revise it regularly. Daily, if needed. But what should your practice plan look like? A practice plan should contain many of the same elements each day but be flexible enough so that you can cut it down to as little as 10 minutes or expand it up to several hours. Each plan should include the following elements: time to listen to a song, a warm-up, goal or goals of the day, a review, and time for fun. (See below for details).

THE 6 STEP PRACTICE PLAN

STEP 1: Listen to a song to get yourself in the right frame of mind. You can listen to a song you're working on, something you've never heard before, or something you've heard hundreds of times. If you have heard it hundreds of times, listen to just the guitar parts. Next time, listen to just the bass, then the drums, then the background vocals or whatever catches your ear. Or listen to something that inspires you, something that makes you want to play. Or listen to a song you already know how to play.

STEP 2: Warm-up. Work on specific scales, exercises, licks, and techniques. (If you aren't sure what to do for a warm-up, be sure to download my free e-book of easy warm-ups: Technique Master: 53 Easy Warm-up Exercises to Revolutionize Your Guitar Playing at TheMissingMethod.com.)

STEP 3: Set your daily goal and start practicing it. If your time is limited, give yourself a reasonable time limit (5-10 minutes). Otherwise, make this portion of your practice session the longest and most involved. Don't forget to use a metronome and add elements of musicality. (You can find metronome apps online if you don't yet have one.)

STEP 4: Review. Review yesterday's goal. Review more recent goals. Again, use a metronome. Add elements of musicality. This should be the second longest part of your practice session.

STEP 5: Play songs you've already memorized. Whenever possible make a list and play every song on the list. Feel free to look things up you may have forgotten and take the time to review it. One of my guitar teachers once told me to put on a one to two hour concert for my cat every day as part of my practice schedule. (My cat loved it; my dog, on the other hand, wasn't a fan. Whenever I hit the distortion pedal, he'd howl.) If you don't have time for that long of a concert, then break it up and do part of it every night, even if it's just one song. For beginners, just do what you can. There's nothing wrong with including exercises into your at-home concert. The cat won't know.

STEP 6: Have Fun. Write your own stuff. Experiment.

To maximize your practice time, you can take your plan a step further and plan out how many minutes (or hours) each step will be. Some guitarists I know go as far as having a timer go off, so they know when to move along. For example, if you have an hour, you could give each section ten minutes. However, it is best to keep your warm-up to about five minutes, and try to keep the work on your main goal the longest part, unless you plan to do a large review. Ultimately, how you structure your time is entirely up to you.

SAMPLE PRACTICE PLAN FOR BEGINNERS

1. **LISTEN:** Listen to the folk song, "House of the Rising Sun."
2. **WARM-UP:** While tapping your foot steadily, review all the notes you've learned to read so far in the method book you are working from.
3. **GOAL OF THE DAY:** Be able to read through the first eight measures of "House of the Rising Sun" found on page 24 of your method book.
4. **REVIEW:** Play "Twinkle, Twinkle Little Star" from yesterday's practice on page 23. Also review the C and G7 chords from page 22. Go back from the beginning of the book and

review all the notes you've learned so far.
5. **RECITAL:** Play the song "Hot Crossed Buns" from page 1 as perfectly as you can. Tap your foot with the beat.
6. **EXPERIMENT:** Using the three chords you already know, write your own chord progression.

SAMPLE PRACTICE PLAN FOR ADVANCED PLAYERS

1. **LISTEN:** Listen to the Wes Montgomery tune Road Song. Pay close attention to the comping (the accompaniment).
2. **WARM-UP:** Do the Monday warm-up, which includes speed drills using the Dorian mode. Also review five Dorian licks.
3. **GOAL OF THE DAY:** Using sheet music, learn the chords for the song Road Song. First review the melody, then start to memorize the chords. The goal is to have the first half of the song memorized.
4. **REVIEW:** Play through the melody of Road Song that you memorized yesterday. Use a metronome or backing track. Play it until you can play it all the way through without a mistake, or until time is up.
5. **RECITAL:** Play through the two songs learned

last week. Use backing tracks or a metronome. Be sure to play all the parts: the tune, the solo, and the rhythm parts. If time, go back and review your entire current list of tunes.
6. **EXPERIMENT:** Using the chords you memorized on Road Song, write out your own licks. Also, try dialing in different pick-up settings and see what blends best with the backing track.

CHAPTER 9 RECAP:

1. Create a practice plan. Be sure to write it down and keep it handy.
2. Revise the plan as often as needed to keep it fresh, fun, and in line with your goals.

Now you try it! Use the worksheet below to figure out your perfect practice plan.

Today's Practice Plan

Date: _____

Listen: _____

Warm-Up: _____

Goal of the Day: _____

Review: _____

Recital: _____

Explore: _____

Reflect: What went well? What do you need to work on? What do you plan to work on tomorrow?

Tip:
Download a copy of this worksheet at:
https://themissingmethod.com/perfect-practice/.

Ideas for Practice

Need practicing ideas? Here are a few to get you started, organized by skill level.

IDEAS FOR BEGINNERS:
- Technique: finger warm-ups, review notes or scales learned, work on picking
- Practice moving from chord to chord
- Memorize chord shapes
- Practice the fingerings for new chords
- Make sure you are using the correct fingering while playing
- Practice strumming with a metronome
- Tap your foot in time (with a metronome

whenever possible).
- Work on note reading and/or TAB reading
- Work on hammer-ons and pull-offs
- Listen to yourself. Do you like the tones your instrument is getting?
- Try writing your own songs based on what you know
- Learn to recognize common patterns in music by ear

IDEAS FOR INTERMEDIATE PLAYERS
- Learn specific rhythms (Discover the differences between AC/DC and The Ramones, for example, or find out what a bossa nova is. How do you play reggae or ska? Find out the differences between be-bop and swing.)
- Techniques: learn sweep picking, learn hybrid picking, find exercises that can help you increase speed and accuracy
- Learn new scales and in different parts of the neck
- Continue to learn and study note reading and music theory
- Continue learning new chords and how to use them in a song
- Experiment with tone

- Try to figure songs out by ear with the assistance of sheet music
- Practice with a metronome and add rhythmic challenges for yourself
- Learn to play styles you aren't that familiar with
- Take time to understand what you are playing (connecting theory to practice)
- Make a list of songs, solos, riffs, or portions of songs you want to learn, or be able to play whole songs, including all the guitar parts

IDEAS FOR ADVANCED PLAYERS
- Learn and study new licks. Play them in every key. Adapt them to your style.
- Learn to play by ear
- Continue to experiment with tone
- Take songs you know well and try to add things to them or take things from them to see how it sounds
- Create your own chord voicings
- Write your own songs and record them if possible
- Learn how to play other instruments like bass, piano, drums, uke, trumpet, etc.
- Use the plethora of guitar books out there to learn how to play like your favorite guitar

players
- Work on more difficult and complicated rhythms
- Master the fretboard; know every note on every string
- Learn new arpeggios
- Take easy exercises and speed them up to neck-break speeds
- Take time to understand what you are playing (connecting theory to practice)
- Make a list of songs, solos, riffs, or portions of songs you want to learn, or be able to play whole songs, including all the guitar parts

Practice Tips:

1. Practice with a metronome
2. Practice with backing tracks (You can record them yourself, use a program like Garage Band to generate them, or find them online, usually YouTube.)
3. Play along with recordings.
4. Record yourself and listen carefully. (Also, you'll discover a great deal about

your playing by recording yourself. If you have any timing issues, you'll find that out pretty quickly).
5. Use books to help you focus. This can also help you measure your progress.
6. Keep things simple, fun, yet always find new challenges to overcome.

Final Thoughts

The practice plan suggested in this book is just that: a suggestion. Everyone works differently and this systematic, ridged approach may not always work for you. However, I am hoping that it will give you ideas, and make you rethink how you practice. If followed exactly as written you will see results. But you must do it every day possible.

The key to perfect practice is *intent*. It's about being consistent, understanding why certain things aren't sounding right, and using what you know to figure out how to correct it.

Most of all, your playing and your practicing should be fun, consistent, and as good as you can make it. Keep it varied. Keep it musical. Keep your standards high. But be sure to enjoy every minute of it.

About the Author

For over 20 years, Christian J. Triola has taught hundreds of students to practice and play guitar. He holds a Master's Degree in Education, a Bachelor's Degree in Music (Jazz Studies), and is the author of over two dozen popular guitar method books. Outside of teaching, he has played in a variety of bands in addition to his many solo performances.

Learn more at TheMissingMethod.com.

Resources to Take Your Playing Further

 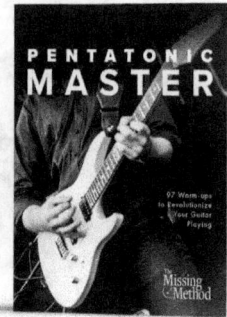 

Avoid injury and learn how to play the right way with the **Technique Master™ Series**. Build finger strength, dexterity, and knowledge of the fretboard with warm-up exercises, scales, licks, arpeggios, and more. Discover the difference a good set of warm-ups can make!

Unlock your musicianship with the power of note reading! **The Missing Method for Guitar™ Note Reading Series** teaches you how to read every note on the guitar, from the open strings to the 22nd fret. If you are looking to master the fretboard, this is the series for you! Available in right and left-handed editions.

***Guitar Chord Master*™** is the only method book series that focuses exclusively on learning chords and strum patterns. Each book takes you step-by-step through the process of learning chords in a musical context, allowing you to master them for life! The series covers open chords, power chords, barre chords, how to use a capo, moveable shapes, and much more. Available in right and left-handed editions.

Find these and more at TheMissingMethod.com

More Tools to Develop Your Skills

Free weekly lessons!

Each week we release videos on a variety of topics from guitar playing basics to music theory, technique, note reading, rhythm practice and more. Join us at https://bit.ly/Missing-Method-YouTube.

Be the first to know . . .
(And get a free gift!)

Our monthly newsletter subscribers are the first to hear of new releases, video lessons and course releases, promotional offers, and more. Join us at TheMissingMethod.com and get a free gift!

www.ingramcontent.com/pod-product-compliance
Lightning Source LLC
Chambersburg PA
CBHW050333120526
44592CB00014B/2170